W9-AMB-726

MYTHICAL CREATURES

SPHINXES

BY THOMAS KINGSLEY TROUPE

BELLWETHER MEDIA • MINNEAPOLIS, MN

Torque brims with excitement
perfect for thrill-seekers of all kinds.
Discover daring survival skills, explore
uncharted worlds, and marvel at mighty
engines and extreme sports. In *Torque* books,
anything can happen. Are you ready?

This edition first published in 2021 by Bellwether Media, Inc.

No part of this publication may be reproduced in whole or in part without written
permission of the publisher.
For information regarding permission, write to Bellwether Media, Inc.,
Attention: Permissions Department, 6012 Blue Circle Drive, Minnetonka, MN 55343.

Library of Congress Cataloging-in-Publication Data

Names: Troupe, Thomas Kingsley, author.
Title: Sphinxes / by Thomas Kingsley Troupe.
Description: Minneapolis, MN : Bellwether Media, Inc., 2021. | Series:
   Torque: mythical creatures | Includes bibliographical references and
   index. | Audience: Ages 7-12 | Audience: Grades 4-6 | Summary: "Amazing
   images accompany engaging information about sphinxes. The combination of
   high-interest subject matter and light text is intended for students in
   grades 3 through 7"– Provided by publisher.
Identifiers: LCCN 2020046778 (print) | LCCN 2020046779 (ebook) | ISBN
   9781644874677 (library binding) | ISBN 9781648341441 (ebook)
Subjects: LCSH: Sphinxes (Mythology)–Juvenile literature.Classification: LCC BL820.
S66 T76 2021 (print) | LCC BL820.S66 (ebook) |
   DDC 398.21–dc23
LC record available at https://lccn.loc.gov/2020046778
LC ebook record available at https://lccn.loc.gov/2020046779

Text copyright © 2021 by Bellwether Media, Inc. TORQUE and associated logos are
trademarks and/or registered trademarks of Bellwether Media, Inc.

Editor: Rebecca Sabelko   Designer: Josh Brink

Printed in the United States of America, North Mankato, MN.

TABLE OF CONTENTS

THE LEGEND OF THE SPHINX

The mountains tower above you. You approach with caution. The sphinx is guarding the mountain pass. It watches your every move. The only way to get through is to answer its tricky riddle.

The sun beats down. The heat makes you feel dizzy. Can you answer its riddle correctly?

Sphinxes have been part of ancient **mythology** for centuries. But little is known about the meaning of these creatures.

Sphinxes often have the body of a lion and the head of a human. They have wings in some **cultures**. Sphinxes often appear as guardians sitting with their heads held high. Some are wise. Others can be tricky or **cruel**.

ANCIENT CREATURES

Great Sphinx of Giza

One of the oldest sphinxes is the Great Sphinx of Giza. This giant limestone statue was carved around 2500 BCE. Some experts believe it has **Pharaoh** Khafra's face.

Sphinx Origin

Egypt =

Other Egyptian sphinxes have been created since the Great Sphinx. But their meaning is unknown. Many historians believe the statues represent royalty.

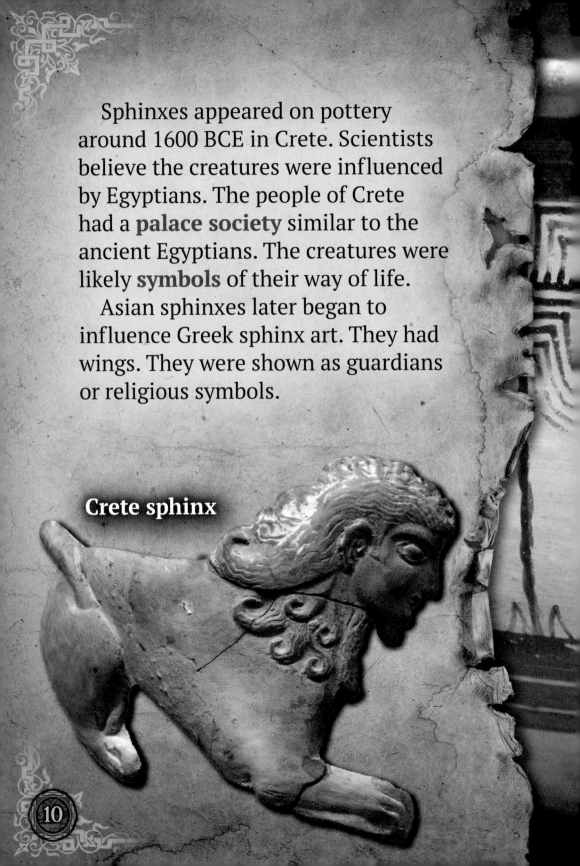

Sphinxes appeared on pottery around 1600 BCE in Crete. Scientists believe the creatures were influenced by Egyptians. The people of Crete had a **palace society** similar to the ancient Egyptians. The creatures were likely **symbols** of their way of life.

Asian sphinxes later began to influence Greek sphinx art. They had wings. They were shown as guardians or religious symbols.

Crete sphinx

sphinx on pottery
from Greece

Assyrian sphinx-like creature

Similar Creatures

Minotaur

mermaid

chimera

faun

Around 700 BCE, sphinxes became more common throughout the **Mediterranean** region. Assyrian and Persian art included statues of bulls with wings and human heads. The statues guarded palaces from evil.

Persian **architecture** later featured the creatures on walls and gates. These sphinxes had male heads. They wore special **headdresses** with horns.

Sphinxes showed up in stories, too. The play *Oedipus the King* tells the tale of a winged sphinx that guarded the city of Thebes. Oedipus wished to enter the city. But the sphinx forced him to answer her riddle.

He answered her riddle correctly. The city was saved, and Oedipus became king.

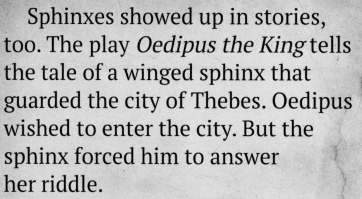

SOLVE THE RIDDLE!

What has four legs in the morning, two at noon, and three in the evening?
(Find the answer on page 22.)

Sphinx Timeline

around 2500 BCE:
The Great Sphinx of Giza
is carved from limestone

around 430 BCE:
The play *Oedipus the
King* is written

**between 400
and 200 BCE:**
Hindu stories of
sphinxes are written

The Hindu **oral tradition** has sphinxes as well. The stories were written between 400 and 200 BCE. One story describes a powerful sphinx that helped the five Pandava brothers keep their kingdom. It tested the brothers' honesty. Their kingdom was protected when they passed the test.

Many temples in India are guarded by sphinxes. They protect the temples from evil. They take **sins** away from visitors.

Purushamriga, the sphinx that helped the Pandavas

STILL A PUZZLE

Today, the most famous sphinx is the Great Sphinx of Giza. Millions of people visit the statue every year. No one knows why it is there. Maybe it is guarding the pharaohs in the nearby pyramids!

Scientists continue to learn about Egyptian sphinxes. A small statue was found in 2018 in a temple near Aswan, Egypt. It is likely more than 2,000 years old!

statue found near Aswan

No More Hairballs

There is a type of hairless cat called sphynx. They are popular with people who are allergic to cats!

Movies and video games sometimes feature sphinxes. The 2016 movie *Gods of Egypt* features a large sphinx made of sand. A sphinx appears in the video game *Super Mario Odyssey*. It asks riddles throughout the game!

These mythical creatures continue to puzzle people around the world!

Media Mention

Book: *Harry Potter and the Goblet of Fire*

Written By: J.K. Rowling

Year Released: 2000

Summary: Harry faces a sphinx in the third task of the Triwizard Tournament and has to answer a riddle to move forward in the maze

Gods of Egypt

GLOSSARY

architecture—the style of a building

cruel—wanting to cause harm

cultures—the beliefs, values, and ways of life of groups of people

headdresses—decorative head coverings

Mediterranean—relating to the Mediterranean Sea and the lands that surround it

mythology—ancient stories about the beliefs or history of a group of people; myths also try to explain events.

oral tradition—spoken customs, ideas, or beliefs handed down from one generation to the next

palace society—an ancient system in which goods are controlled by a palace or ruler; in palace societies, the people give goods to the ruler who then decides how much is given back.

pharaoh—a ruler of ancient Egypt

sins—actions that break religious rules

symbols—things that stand for something else

THE RIDDLE SOLVED!

The answer to the riddle on page 14 is a human! A human walks on four legs as a baby, two as an adult, and three as an elder with a cane.

TO LEARN MORE

AT THE LIBRARY

Honovich, Nancy. *1,000 Facts About Ancient Egypt.* Washington, D.C.: National Geographic, 2019.

Lawrence, Sandra, and Stuart Hill. *The Atlas of Monsters: Mythical Creatures from Around the World.* Philadelphia, Pa.: Running Press Kids, 2019.

Sautter, A.J. *Discover Harpies, Minotaurs, and Other Mythical Fantasy Beasts.* North Mankato, Minn.: Capstone Press, 2018.

ON THE WEB

FACTSURFER

Factsurfer.com gives you a safe, fun way to find more information.

1. Go to www.factsurfer.com

2. Enter "sphinxes" into the search box and click 🔍.

3. Select your book cover to see a list of related content.

INDEX

The images in this book are reproduced through the courtesy of: Eric Isselee, front cover (lion), p. 5 (lion); Sanit Fuangnakhon, front cover (wings); tommasco lizzul, front cover (face); Leon Rafael, front cover (background); Vixit, p. 3 (background); N. Rotteveel, p. 3 (figure); Santhosh Varghese, p. 5 (hiker); faestock, p. 5 (face); jakkapan, p. 5 (wings); Brenda Kean/ Alamy, pp. 6-7; Olaf Krüger/ Alamy, pp. 6-7, 13 (bottom left); AlexAnton, pp. 8-9; Zde/ Wiki Commons, pp. 10, 10-11; B.O'Kane/ Alamy, pp. 12-13; Artur Balytskyi/ Alamy p. 13 (top left); Science History Images/ Alamy, pp. 13 (top right), 15 (middle); Albatross/ Alamy, p. 13 (bottom right); Ivy Close Images/ Alamy, p. 14; Daily Travel Photos, p. 15 (top); Rajadeekshitar/ Wiki Commons, p. 15 (bottom); Historic Collection/ Alamy, pp. 16-17; Hari Prasad Nadig/ Wiki Commons, p. 17; otsphoto, pp. 18-19; Xinhua/ Newscom, pp. 18-19; mohd kamarul hafiz, p. 20; TCD/Prod.DB/ Alamy, pp. 20-21; Alexander Izmaylov, pp. 22-24.